Kitschy Cocktails

Luscious Libations

for the

Swinger Set

Babs Harrison

SMITHMARK

Text copyright © 1999 by Babs Harrison.

This edition published in 1999 by SMITHMARK Publishers, a division of U.S. Media Holdings, Inc., 115 West 18th Street, New York, NY 10011.

SMITHMARK books are available for bulk purchase for sales and promotion and premium use. For details write or call the manager of special sales, SMITHMARK Publishers, 115 West 18th Street, New York, NY 10011; 212-519-1300.

Kitschy Cocktails is produced by becker&mayer!, Kirkland, Washington. www.beckermayer.com

From the *Kitschy Cocktails* packaged set, which includes paper drink umbrellas, swizzle sticks, and this book.

Design by Heidi Baughman
Production by Amy Sinclair
Edited by Lissa Wolfendale

Section opener art pages 14, 28, 38, 46, 50, 56 copyright © 1999 by Peter Georgeson. Cover photography by Michels Advertising Photography. Drink styled by Amy Muzyka-McGuire, R.D. Selected clip art copyright © 1997 Ad Graphics, Retro Ad Art.

ISBN: 0-7651-0818-6

Printed and manufactured in Hong Kong

10 9 8 7 6 5 4 3 2 1

Table of Contents

Introduction

*H*as the beer keg left you flat? Tired of those snobby stemmed wines and their poseur crowd? If you're the type whose heartbeat quickens to a blender's roar or your foot starts tapping to the syncopating rhythm of the cocktail shaker, you're still waiting for the second coming of Don the Beachcomber or prostrate yourself in front of the graven image of Victor "Trader Vic" Bergeron—patron saint of tropical kitsch—then kitschy cocktails are for you!

If this is your first flirtation with tropical kitsch and even if you have hitherto been "cocktail-challenged," follow us: We'll be your Moscow Muled–Kitschy Cocktail Muse on this alcoholic rite of passage. Whether an occasional imbiber or a perennial lounge lizard, you'll find kitschy cocktails are always party-friendly. And, if you have enough of these oft colorfully bright drinks, you just might figure out what to do with that paper umbrella that pokes you in the eye every time you take a sip.

Don't dawdle—every day you wait means one less cocktail hour to enjoy. Upon taking that hallowed shaker rhythmically in hand, you might just discover that the kitschy cocktail party isn't a lost art at all, but rather a newfound profession…yours! The proof, from 80 to 151, is in the glass. So grab a Scorpion (the drink, silly) and follow us to Shangri-la, as we help you transcend your hum-drum world and rise toward the kick-back, party-down, bongo-drum paradise of the urban luau….

The Kitschy Cocktail Muse Manifesto:

The Kitschy Cocktail Muse will now lay down her ten commandments, which of course you'll break. But don't say she didn't tell you so.

Kitschy Cocktail Rule #1: Thou Shalt Not Overmix or Overmingle

While you will want to experiment, you don't need to genetically re-engineer the tropical drink. We've included tried and true recipes, drawn from a careful balance of liquor, fruit juice, and sweetener, for you to memorize and clone for a party. Longing to boldly go where no mixologist has gone before? Remember your first paint set: Mix too many colors and you'll end up with murky brown gook. Fruit liqueurs are especially tempting with their bright colors and exotic fragrances. They are the malcontents of the tropical cocktail world, wanting to jump into every swimming pool of gin. You must exhibit restraint. A little goes a long, long way. Always remember: If you fall off that barstool in mixology training, get right back up and try again!

Kitschy Cocktail Rule #2: Thou Shalt Learn to Shake, Stir, and Blend, But Not All in the Same Drink

There is a reason the Muse recommends a drink be either violently shaken, softly stirred in a clockwise pattern, or electrically blended. Each process alters the flavor of the drink.

Stirring gently mixes without bruising liqueurs (or your knuckles). The shaking process flecks off tiny bits of ice into the drink and renders it icy cold. Blending liquefies and creates a fab slush, such as a banana daiquiri, but timing is crucial: Blending too long will water down the drink, spoiling its carefully engineered structure. You will usually shake or blend cloudy or creamy drinks, and stir clear drinks.

Kitschy Cocktail Rule #3: Thou Shalt Perform in Front of Thy Guests

The silver shaker is your entrée to bartender fame, so adapt your own signature antics. Don't be afraid to practice in front of a full-length mirror to voodoo lounge music. In *The Thin Man* Nick Charles says, "A Manhattan should be shaken to a fox-trot, the Bronx to a two-step, but a dry martini must always be shaken to a waltz." Pick your tune and shake things up.

Kitschy Cocktail Rule #4: Thou Shalt Not Run Out of Liquor

Nothing kills a party faster than running out of liquor. Your thirsty muse shall desert you in the wake of such an embarrassing spectacle.

To ensure that the bar runs smoothly, choose only one or two specialty drinks that show off your newfound skills as the mad, bad mixologist, and supplement them with the more monastic stirred drinks. For example, you might choose to serve one blender drink, say a piña colada, and an easy rum drink, such as a rum and tonic. Have a bottle of gin on the bar, and you can easily toss together gin and tonics. You get the picture.

Kitschy Cocktail Rule #5: Thou Shalt Decorate the Drinks, the Den, Thyself

Turn your pad into an ersatz Cocoanut Grove or a personal Tiki Lounge. The goal is to transport your guests to a heated tropical locale where they are refreshed by superb icy drinks.

Have plastic pink flamingoes cavort amongst tiki torches on the lawn. Transform the wood-paneled den with scary Polynesian masks and statues (think Easter Island), conch shells, and faux palm trees or fronds sprouting from the corners. Anything bamboo will help the nouveau tropical lounge lizard feel at home.

Kitschy Cocktail Rule #6: Thou Shalt Play Music

Anything by Don Ho is perfect, as are Tiki cocktail lounge recordings, Hawaiian guitar, and Tahitian drum music—you want to encourage the wiggling of hips. How about kicky Latin tunes? A little Sinatra and Louis Prima from the '50s? Evoke a true cocktail lounge with sultry sirens such as Julie "Cry Me a River" London, or crooners Dean Martin and Vic Damone.

Kitschy Cocktail Rule #7: Thou Shalt Not Be Boring, Whether Guest or Host

The Muse puts down her spiked mule heel on this point. No bores, whiners, or prissy types allowed at urban luaus. If you can't cut loose, go home and cut the grass instead.

For a truly lively party, create a guest list as if you were mixing a cocktail—blend something strong with something fruity, accent with something sweet, and top with something unexpected. So call up those drinking dilettantes, debutantes, subdebs and near-debs, dewy-faced ingenues, friends and acquaintances, a poseur or two, and a cad of questionable character.

The number of guests you invite depends on whether you prefer an elbow-to-elbow crowd or perhaps something more intimate around the pool, say no more than twenty bikinis? If you have removed all breakables, by all means *do* cram the living room. Otherwise, cull the list to a manageable few, especially if your supplies amount to one bottle of rum and a bag of Cheetos.

Kitschy Cocktail Rule #8: Thou Shalt Be a Snappy Host

You, the consummate host, should always appear nattily dressed, somewhat playful but never frazzled—even if your Lava Flow specialty is causing a *petit* eruption in the kitchen—and quick with a witticism, an off-color joke, or a stupid bar trick, whichever the occasion calls for. Think Tanqueray's Mr. Jenkins goes to the Poconos.

At a loss for style? Emulate a famous cocktail host. Consider Dean Martin (can you drape yourself over a piano and slide off without spilling your drink?) or one of the other stars of the Rat Pack. Do heed Dorothy Parker's famous martini ditty: "I love a good martini, two at the most; three I'm under the table, four I'm under the host." If you get to five, you may continue this poem and post it on the Web.

Your duties include meeting and greeting each guest, generously replenishing drinks, and ensuring all guests are amusing themselves wildly. Short of cloning yourself and several sheep named Dolly who can mix drinks, this will be tricky. Engage a friend (but don't marry them) to cohost or help with the duties. Strive for a spirit of relaxed gaiety at your party, at least until it falls into depraved debauchery.

Party paranoia and cocktail crises are not in the Snappy Host's repertoire, for Snappy Host remembers the reason for the party— to visit with friends, show off, alter friends' personalities with delicious cocktails so they will spill secrets, and witness indiscretions both physical and verbal among said cocktail companions for supreme Monday morning water cooler gossip.

Kitschy Cocktail Rule #9: Thou Shalt Not Overindulge Thyself or Thy Guests

Indulge your guests, but do not overindulge yourself: Etiquette demands that the Snappy Host stay somewhat sober. There's a fine line between passing out and going to sleep, and one too many kitschy cocktails is sure to erase it. You don't want to personify Between-the-Sheets—it's meant to be served to your guests. Your cocktail companions may slowly lose control, being way past total recall come morning, but the host *always* remembers.

Kitschy Cocktail Rule #10: Thou Shalt Not Covet Thy Neighbor's Bar

Get your own damn bar. If you live in a '50s ranchburger, you probably have a built-in bar complete with Naugahyde bar stools. If not, pity. You'll have to build a shrine to the cocktail. A pyramid in the backyard might be amusing (upside-down martini glasses), or perhaps a few shelves and a corner of the kitchen counter will do.

Essential Urban Luau Barware and Ingredients

*U*se the following as guidelines for setting up your very own kitschy cocktail bar.

- **Bar spoon.** You could use grandmother's silver iced tea spoon—it's long enough for stirring cocktails in deep glasses, but a real bar spoon has a larger bowl.
- **A blender.** This is one of the best investments you can make in your life as a kitschy cocktail bartender. Don't skimp here. Go for the high-powered master, preferably one that also crushes ice. Muse knows, a bartender is only as good as her equipment allows her to be.
- **Cocktail napkins.** These must be decorated with an appropriate motif, and may be changed as the party progresses. "It's past our bedtime, won't you please go home" can be handed out with the final round of drinks to encourage cocktail companions to slouch toward home. Of course, that's assuming your guests can still read at that point.
- **Cutting board.** This, plus a very sharp knife, for slicing fruit.
- **Fresh fruit for garnish.** You can't overdo it here, so just let your creative side go. Think Carmen Miranda on a toothpick. The gaudier the better. See "Garnished Inspiration," page 13, for more details.
- **A glacier.** Ice is American—a sign of wealth, power, and abundance. You need your very own mountain of ice that can be chipped and crushed as needed. Park that glacier outside the back door and don't be stingy.

- Glasses. Hollowed-out coconuts and pineapples may be substituted for barware—this will render you totally cool. For some of you, the glass situation might pose a problem. Muse suspects your containers might bear the logos and cute sayings of god-only-knows what. Solution: Get a life. For party glasses, buy disposable tall, clear plastic cups or rent glasses: A tall tumbler (called highball or collins in 8- or 12-ounce sizes) for the tropical drinks, and a stemmed glass for daiquiris, martinis, stingers, and other classics should do the trick.

- Ice bucket. Very handy for keeping ice at hand so you're not continually emptying ice trays. These come in various guises, from football and Viking helmets to images of tiki monoliths. Check your dad's attic or ask Mom which Goodwill store she gave it to.

- Ice scoop. A must for scooping crushed and cubed ice.

- Shaker (in case yours is missing, it comes with a lid). This is the distinguishing feature of your well-equipped tropical bar. There are two styles of shakers: a mixing glass with a stainless steel top held over the top, or the very deco-looking silver bullet. You can use a large iced tea glass and plastic top from a Cool Whip container. However, this is very un-swank.

- A strainer with spring coil. Very professional looking. Place on top of steel shaker to strain cocktails so stuff doesn't get into the glass.

- Jiggers. Bartending is a science—liquid alchemy, mixology—so measurements are rather important if you don't have the professional pourers screwed onto the liquor bottles. Your blender will also have measurements for mixing massive amounts of chemical warfare.

- **Liquor.** The key to a great kitschy party is lots of liquor. Count on three drinks per person, unless all your friends are lushes...okay, so make it four. A fifth (750 ml) of liquor, pouring 1½ ounces per drink, should serve seventeen people. If you're messy, spill a lot, or overserve, count on ten drinks.
- **A muddler.** This wooden pestle is better than your thumb for grinding sugar cubes into Angostura bitters and the like.
- **Swizzle sticks.** Brightly colored, these treasured props come in the shape of hanging monkeys, Caribbean women, exotic birds, palm trees, and sharks, among others. Guests will either chew on them during a conversation lull, a sure sign that more drinks are needed—or they will pocket them, the ultimate compliment.
- **Plastic straws.** Use these, in bright colors and crazy shapes, when all your swizzle sticks have been lifted.
- **Paper Japanese umbrellas.** Don't let a drink leave the bar without at least one. Placed in the open position, please, they instantly say kitschy cocktail!
- **Deliciously messy tropical fruit syrups and juices,** depending on the chosen drink recipes. Fresh fruit juices are preferred.
- **Squeezer or juicer.** For fresh juice; you weren't thinking of buying that bottled stuff, were you? Muse doth protest.

Garnished Inspiration

𝒯he cocktail's crowning glory is the fruitful garnish that elicits a cheery spirit of the tropics, with all the colorful and immodest splendor of a drag queen. Ay caramba!

- Maraschino cherries, laced shish-kebab style, onto a frilly pick. Use all red, all green, or mix the two.
- An orange, lime, or kiwi wheel speared with a cherry. Try sliding a green cherry next to the red one. Ooh la la.
- An umbrella speared onto a cherry and an orange wheel, all perched on the rim of a glass.
- A smallish orchid blossom on a pick, speared into any fruit garnish.
- Two (one is a lonely number) pimento-stuffed green olives speared onto a frilly toothpick and dropped into a martini.
- A pineapple spear, sliced lengthwise, serves as swizzle stick and can be topped with a red cherry and an orchid.
- A spiral of orange or lemon peel (this will take some sober attention to perfect). Allow "tail" to dangle outside glass. Add umbrella and swizzle stick.
- A stacked garnish: Take a long, slim swizzle stick or long toothpick and skewer on a variety of fruit—cherries, pineapple wedges, coconut slices—with an orchid on the top.

Rum

$\mathcal{T}$his is the cool daddy of tropical fun, the quintessential fuel of the tropics, whose origins began with that infamous Italian Christopher Columbus. He introduced sugarcane to Puerto Rico in the fifteenth century, which in turn produced rum, as rum is made from the sap of the sugarcane (distilled from molasses left after the sugar has boiled out). Rum became the drink of sailors and pirates on the high seas, and many a sailor in the eighteenth century was paid in rum (imagine an employer trying that today).

Escaping Prohibition in 1920, America's thirsty fled to rum-soaked Cuba where island bartenders invented a fabulous repertoire of tropical drinks. Americans proceeded to get wasted in the tropics throughout the '20s and '30s. For those who stayed home, Puerto Rican rum became extremely popular on the mainland during World War II, when American distillers were required to produce more industrial alcohol for the war effort and much less alcohol for drinking.

Fashion-conscious bartenders take note: Rum is available in a variety of shades. Dark and golden rums are aged in charred oak casks, sometimes with the addition of caramel; clear or white rum has been stored in stainless tanks. Numerous recipes will mix rums, and some call for an optional 151 (read: extremely flammable) "floater" for an added kick start. You'll find that rum, especially the heavy, dark, Jamaican variety, mixes delightfully with fruit juices and syrups, as it can definitely hold its own. But don't go overboard; mix one too many an accessory with rum and your guests will jump ship.

Daiquiri

*T*he beauty of a daiquiri in Muse's oft muddled mind is that you need only three easily accessible ingredients: light rum, fresh lime, and sugar. Shake, rattle, and roll them into a beautifully chilled cocktail glass and *voilà!* Instant panache with a lime garnish.

Hemingway drank (a lot of) these in Cuba. His favorite bar, La Floridita, invented the Hemingway Special for him. A variation on the daiquiri, it called for 1½ ounces light rum, juice of half a lime, ¼ ounce grapefruit juice, and ¼ ounce maraschino liqueur mixed with ice. Today's literary wanna-bes might try this version to incite inspiration.

> 1¼ ounces light rum
> juice of ½ lime
> ½ teaspoon sugar

Shake in shaker with ice, and strain into a chilled cocktail glass. Garnish with lime. To create a slush drink, blend the recipe with crushed ice in a blender with 4 large, fresh strawberries or ½ banana, and decrease juice to ¼ lime.

Lanai Daiquiri

*T*here's nothing like a little pineapple to kitsch up a classic. For this, we go to the source of the world's tastiest pineapple, Hawaii. The island of Lanai, formerly known as the Pineapple Isle, once grew 20,000 acres of pineapple garnish.

But cocktails went out of favor, pineapples grew cheaper (but not as flavorful) elsewhere, and well, that's what happens when you don't throw enough cocktail parties with pineapple garnish. Let's hope the same fate does not befall the maraschino cherry isle. Lanai is now home to two super-swank resorts, one of which, The Lodge at Koele bar—craftily called The Tea Room—created this homage to the pine. It's warmed up many an upcountry cool night. And you may share the wealth; this recipe provides for several guests. Room keys not provided.

1 fresh vanilla bean, preferably from Tahiti
1 fresh pineapple, pared and quartered
1 bottle Myers's dark rum
1 bottle Bacardi light rum
1 bottle Bacardi dark rum
handful of brown sugar cubes
handful of white sugar cubes

Slit and strip the vanilla bean: With a sharp knife, slit the bean anywhere down the middle. Pull the bean apart and scrape the seeds out. Add all ingredients, including the bean, into a large (gallon) container, ensuring that the pineapple is covered with rum. Allow to marinate in refrigerator for 48 hours. Remove the pineapple and cut into wedges. Stir liquid to combine sugar and pineapple juice, and pour into a chilled cocktail glass, garnished with a rum-soaked pineapple wedge.

Mai Tai

Muse orders a mai tai as soon as her plane touches down in Hawaii and she has wiggled into her itsy-bitsy bikini. The Royal Hawaiian, that pink honeymoon cabana of cabanas on Waikiki, is famous for these lascivious potions (and the view of Diamond Head isn't bad either).

But truly, the mai tai was invented by none other than our cherished Tiki god, Victor Bergeron, way back in the '40s at his restaurant in Oakland, California. The name came from the words of a Tahitian customer, unsuspecting guinea pig to mai tai history, who, upon tasting the just-invented drink, exclaimed "Mai tai...roe ae," meaning "Out of this world...the best." And it really is.

2 ounces light rum
1 ounce Jamaican or dark rum
½ ounce curaçao or other orange liqueur
½ ounce orgeat or other almond syrup
½ ounce lemon or lime juice

Half-fill a large goblet with crushed ice. Add light rum, Jamaican rum, curaçao, orgeat, and lemon or lime juice. Fill glass with more crushed ice and stir contents gently. Garnish with a sprig of mint, a pineapple slice, and a maraschino cherry.

Paddler's Passion

This fab drink is the signature libation at the open-air Canoe House bar and restaurant at Mauna Lani Bay on the Big Island of Hawaii. The Hawaiian bartenders serve this lethal mixture in an innocent-looking, hollowed-out pineapple. Barring that you have a pineapple plantation, use a tall glass. A few of these, and you'll be paddling without a paddle.

1 ounce Bacardi amber rum
1 ounce vodka
1½ ounces passion fruit juice
1½ ounces orange juice
dash of coconut syrup
dash of grenadine

Mix all ingredients in blender with shaved ice (crushed ice will do). Blend and pour into a scooped-out whole pineapple, replace top, and serve with a straw. Garnish with a wedge of pineapple and a cherry.

Blue Hawaii

Famous bartender (hey, you could be famous too some day for behind-the-bar antics) Harry Yee created this potion in Waikiki in the '50s, and Elvis made the movie. In fact, did you know that every time there's an Elvis sighting, he's drinking Blue Hawaii? Join the King and be blue, but don't step on my blue-suede shoe. Oh gee, that's not your shoe?

2 ounces pineapple juice

1 ounce light rum

1 ounce coconut cream

1 ounce blue curaçao

Combine pineapple juice, rum, coconut cream, and curaçao with crushed ice in blender, and mix well. Pour into a glass, and garnish with a wedge of pineapple, a strip of coconut, and a cherry. Serve with a straw, sip, and watch for Elvis.

Lava Flow

This daily occurrence at the Four Seasons Wailea on Maui comes not from a volcano but from the bar (the last real lava flow on Maui was in 1790). Indeed, the resourceful bartenders at this resort invented a drink the color of oozing lava, and perhaps after several, you'll experience an eruption in your head. It must be a pleasurable one, for the Lava Flow is the most popular drink requested by guests. These adult cream pops glide down as easily as lava slides down a volcano.

1¼ ounces light rum

½ banana

2 ounces colada mix (pineapple juice and coconut syrup)

1 ounce liquid ice cream

¼ cup strawberry purée

Blend rum, banana, colada mix, and ice cream. Pour strawberry purée into a glass about ⅓ full, then pour blended mixture over the top to create a swirl.

Tai Chi

A form of martial art, tai chi in kitschy bar-speak is a drink created by a certain bartender with a black belt. The hands-down most popular drink at Stevenson's Library at the Hyatt Regency Poipu, Kauai, it combines the best of a mai tai and a chi chi. Twenty thousand customers a year can't be wrong. This is the cocktail to effect an instant transformation from gawky weenie to graceful, slow-moving tai chi master. Kick back and tai one on!

> ½ ounce Malibu rum
> ½ ounce Captain Morgan rum
> ¼ ounce orgeat
> ¼ ounce orange curaçao
> dash sweet and sour
> dash pineapple or orange juice
> splash of Bacardi 151 rum

Mix first six ingredients in a 12-ounce glass with ice cubes. Float Bacardi 151 rum over ice. Garnish with a vanda orchid.

Hulopo'e Punch

*W*hen those Jamaican drinks have you feeling a bit heavy, go lighter, mon. This light rum punch was created by a bartender at the Manele Bay Hotel, a snazzy little hideaway overlooking Hulopo'e Bay on the island of Lanai. A punch will ensure smooth sailing, but don't let the light rum deceive you, for an optional "floater" is the surprise attack in the water. Go for it!

¾ ounce light Bacardi rum

½ ounce curaçao

2 ounces orange juice

3 ounces Dole pineapple juice

splash of grenadine

splash of 151 Bacardi rum

Mix first five ingredients and pour over ice. Float with Bacardi 151 rum. Garnish with a pineapple wedge and an orchid.

Jump Up and Kiss Me

*W*hen your party starts to lag, Muse suggests serving these. Snappy host will, of course, recite the name of the drink before serving, and you'll subsequently get a kiss or not. No kiss, no drink. No sense of humor. Why did you invite these people anyway? Have one yourself. After all, if you can't love yourself, who will?

1¼ ounces Myers's dark rum

4 ounces pineapple juice

½ ounce Rose's lime juice

dash Angostura bitters

Shake with ice, and serve over ice.

Cuba Libre

*I*t's Cuba Libre, not Libra—that's Muse's astrological sign. When sent to Cuba sans alcohol in the late nineteenth century to drive out the Spaniards, American soldiers (ever resourceful when the chips are down) mixed the local rum with their rations of Coca-Cola. The boys named the drink after a battle cry heard at the front: "Cuba libre!" A nice story, but one could also say this drink was named for Cuba in the '20s where people were free to drink, unlike America where Prohibition was being enforced. Whichever story fits the current cocktail patter, you, the snappy host, are free to use. For a less sweet drink, substitute tonic water for cola. For a Black Buck, use ginger ale with lemon instead of lime. As every good bartender knows, keep your options open.

1¾ ounces light rum
4 ounces Coca-Cola
juice of ¼ lime

Pour rum into a tall glass filled with ice. Fill with cola, add lime juice, and stir. Garnish with a slice of lime.

Planter's Punch

*T*he most enduring of rum cocktails, this sweet and potent drink has been around in one form or another since the seventeenth century. There are oodles of variations, and Muse is sure you will come up with your very own delish combo, won't you?

2 ounces Jamaican dark rum
1 ounce lemon or lime juice
3 ounces orange juice
1 teaspoon grenadine

Shake with ice cubes. Strain, and serve in a tumbler with cubes. Garnish with orange slice and maraschino cherry.

Between-the-Sheets

*T*his blend of rum and brandy is sure to cause an "under-cover" scandal—unless you're there by yourself, in which case you're just boring, and that is definitely not allowed at urban luaus. Protect or enhance your questionable reputation and always make this "cocktails for two." And do make sure the sheets are clean.

¼ ounce rum
¼ ounce triple sec
¼ ounce brandy
juice of ½ lemon

Shake cracked ice with rum, triple sec, brandy, and lemon juice in shaker. Strain into a chilled, sugar-rimmed cocktail glass, and garnish with a twist of lemon or lime peel.

Piña Colada

*A*dult slurpees for the beach bunny set, these creamy drinks are the perennial vacation accessory. If you like piña coladas, play Rupert Holmes's '78 hit "Escape...the Piña Colada Song." Who knows, you might find your coco loco escape is closer than you imagined. Imagine.

1½ ounces light rum
1 ounce pineapple juice
1 ounce coconut milk
½ ounce cream
1 hollowed-out coconut (nice but optional)

Combine cracked ice with rum, pineapple juice, coconut milk, and cream in shaker, and shake until frosty (the drink, not you). Strain into a hollowed-out coconut or a large glass. Garnish with a maraschino cherry and a wedge of pineapple. Serve with a straw.

Three Barrels of Monkeys

*W*hat could be more fun than a barrel of monkeys? Why, three barrelsful, of course! Mix up barrels of this sensationally good drink, and don't be surprised if your guests start monkeying around.

   1 ounce Myers's dark rum
   ¼ ounce banana liqueur
   ¼ ounce Irish Cream

Pour over ice, and stir.

Bermuda Triangle

*T*he legend persists that ships, intrepid explorers, and wayward tourists can get sucked right into this beautiful triangular space of blue water around Bermuda and never be found again. A simpler solution to getting lost is to suck down one too many of these. You may have to traipse to Bermuda for a bottle of Bermuda Gold, a delicious liqueur made from island loquats, but what a small price to pay for a truly tasty cocktail.

1 ounce Gosling's Black Seal rum (preferred, but any
   dark rum will do)
1 ounce Bermuda Gold
4 ounces orange or pineapple juice

Shake with ice and pour into a tall glass with ice cubes.

Gombey Smash

Colorful costumes and whirling dance are not required, but may be a side effect of this Carnival cocktail. The Gombeys know how to party, mon, so follow their lead and have a smashing time.

½ ounce Cocksbear rum (or other dark rum)
½ ounce Bacardi white rum
½ ounce Creme de Banana
½ ounce Malibu coconut rum
4 ounces pineapple juice
dash Angostura Bitters
dash grenadine syrup

Shake and pour over ice cubes. Party on.

Bongo Drum

Are those drums I hear? From across the river? No, they're somewhat closer. In my head? Yes, all those many, many Bongo Drums are most definitely drumming in my head, forcing me to bongo across the den and go where no bartender has gone before...early to bed.

1 ounce Bacardi light rum
4 ounces pineapple juice
¼ ounce blackberry-flavored brandy

Pour rum into a tall glass filled with ice. Fill with pineapple juice. Float the brandy on top.

Pink Paradise

*W*hen you're in paradise, you're in the pink. Something about those pink sunsets, pink flowers, pink aloha shirts. Wait, are those pink elephants? Better have another before the pink Cadillac comes to take you away.

1½ ounces coconut rum
1 ounce amaretto
3 ounces cranberry juice
1½ ounces pineapple juice

Combine ingredients over ice in a tall glass. Garnish with a pineapple wedge and a cherry.

Vodka

*W*ho would guess something odorless, colorless, and practically tasteless could pack such a wallop? Like the friendly homecoming queen—pure but not so innocent—vodka successfully imprints with just about anything. No snappy host should be without a bottle in the freezer.

Word is that vodka was developed in Russia in the fourteenth century, and indeed the Russians have a fine appreciation for this spirit once distilled from potatoes but nowadays mostly from grains. Muse thinks neat shots of vodka served with caviar is positively decadent and should be enjoyed often.

All vodkas are distilled at a high proof, and most are filtered through activated charcoal to further remove any semblance of flavor. Many import vodkas now are naturally flavored with lemon, pepper, pineapple, and berries. Believe it or not, American law stipulates that its vodkas must be produced with no color, taste, or odor. A strange law indeed for a beverage, but in this puritanical country, guess what the number one selling distilled spirit is?

Vodka, of course, does have its place. It was introduced to the U.S. in the 1930s as a key ingredient in a drink called the Moscow Mule, served in a copper cup. Notorious vodka drinks include the Bloody Mary, the Screwdriver, and the two Russians (White and Black). Vodka's mixability is simply legendary.

Cosmopolitan Martini

*Y*ears ago, yours truly put on her high heels (with little black dress) and sipped her first Cosmo at the oh-so-swank Four Seasons Hotel bar in New York. This pink martini, which my classic martini father would find abhorrent, was served in a swimming pool of a glass, and Muse dove right in. What with all that intoxicating I.M. Pei design and New York style, Muse has loved them ever since. In fact, her home is known around the neighborhood as Salon Cosmo, so do drop in if you're in the pink to party. Now if Mr. Pei could only design a teensy pyramid for my bar….

> 1½ ounces Cointreau or Triple Sec
> 3 ounces vodka
> juice of ½ lime
> splash cranberry juice

Shake with ice and strain into a chilled glass. Garnish with lime twist.

Blue Lagoon

*P*eer over the rim into this blue lagoon and you'll have visions of paradise hula-dancing in your head. Wait! Are those shark fins cutting through the rippling waves? Oh, never mind—it's just the cherries bobbing among the ice cubes.

> 1 ounce vodka
> 1 ounce blue curaçao
> 6 ounces lemonade

Pour vodka and curaçao into a 16-ounce ice-filled goblet. Stir, and fill with lemonade. Decorate with 3 maraschino cherries, and serve with a straw.

Chi Chi

Several chi chis and you'll begin to cha-cha across the carpet. Place little umbrellas behind your ears and cut up the rug. Chi-ky keen.

  - 1½ ounces vodka
  - 1 ounce coconut cream
  - 4 ounces unsweetened pineapple juice

Place cracked ice in blender. Add vodka, coconut cream, and pineapple juice. Blend for 10 seconds only. Strain into a large glass. Garnish with a maraschino cherry and a pineapple wedge. Serve with a straw.

Moscow Mule

Despite the fact that Muse bears not a trace of Russian blood, save for the fine Russian vodka coursing through her veins, the Moscow Mule is a worthy namesake. It appears demure, but delivers quite a kick. It was a wildly successful drink, concocted in California and served in a smart copper mug. Muse recalls her parents kept two Moscow Mule copper mugs on top of the refrigerator and out of reach of Baby Muse. Luckily, the little girl's grown....

1½ ounces vodka
4 ounces ginger beer
juice of ½ lime

Pour vodka into a mug, preferably copper, over ice cubes. Add lime juice and fill with ginger beer. Stir and drop a lime wedge into the mug for garnish.

Salty Dog

*T*otally refreshing on those dog-day afternoons, this drink will have guests pawing you for more. Perhaps you can teach them new tricks. Perhaps not.

salt and lemon juice to frost glass
1½ ounces vodka
grapefruit juice

Pour vodka over ice cubes into a salt-rimmed, tall glass. Fill with grapefruit juice. Garnish with a wedge of lemon.

Bikini

A two-piece sensation named after the atoll in the Pacific where the bomb was tested—or was some naughty bartender shaking his shaker without a lid? In any case, these fancy drinks are sure to turn your party into a blast. Stand back when this baby is being shaken.

2 ounces vodka
juice of ½ lemon

1 ounce white rum
½ ounce milk
1 teaspoon sugar

Pour vodka, lemon juice, white rum, milk, and sugar over ice in shaker. Shake until frosty. Strain into a cocktail glass. Garnish with a lemon twist.

Surf Rider

Can you hang ten, surfer dude? What, never surfed before in your life? Then you'll need several of these, my friend. Surf's up!

3 ounces vodka
1 ounce sweet vermouth
juice of 1 orange
juice of ½ lemon
½ teaspoon grenadine

Pour vodka, vermouth, fruit juices, and grenadine over cracked ice in shaker. Shake until frosty. Strain into a glass. Garnish with three maraschino cherries. Serve with a straw.

Harvey Wallbanger

This legend recounts the tale of a '60s surfer named Harvey who drank vodka and Galliano to get over wiping-out in a surfing tournament. Two of these and Harvey would start banging his head against walls. Would you want a drink like this named after you?

1 ounce vodka
4 ounces orange juice
½ ounce Galliano

Pour vodka and orange juice into a collins glass filled with ice cubes. Stir. Float Galliano on top.

Hawaii Five-0

*P*ut on the theme music to this wildly popular TV show of a few years back, toast to the memory of McGarrett played by the inimitable Jack Lord, and go up to someone and say, "Book 'im, Danno!" Don't call Muse with your one phone call from jail.

1½ ounces Finlandia pineapple vodka
¼ ounce blue curaçao

Shake, and serve in a chilled cocktail glass with ice. Garnish with a pineapple spear, a cherry, and an umbrella.

Sex on the Beach

*M*use can just hear the response when you innocently ask for one of these: "This right here is prohibited in America, so you just leave on all those clothes of yours, ya hear?" Well, the next best thing is sex in a glass. Enough of these and you'll feel the sand between your wiggling toes.

1 ounce vodka
¼ ounce Chambord

¼ ounce Midori
1 ounce pineapple juice

Combine in a shaker. Shake or stir. Serve straight up or over ice.

Crocodile Cooler

*G*o croco. Slither around with a skin worth thousands of green-backs. As a perennial lounge lizard, you should have no problem here. But the real question is, can you gator?

1½ ounces citrus vodka
1 ounce melon liqueur
¾ ounce triple sec
2 ounces sour mix
4 ounces lemon-lime soda

Place first four ingredients in a parfait or hurricane glass filled with ice cubes. Fill with soda, and stir well. Garnish with a pineapple wedge and a cherry or a lime wheel. Serve with a straw.

Jungle Juice

*I*t's a jungle out there, so why not party with the animals? This is sure to loosen up the most homebound of domestic creatures.

    1 ounce vodka
    1 ounce rum
    ½ ounce triple sec
    1 splash sour mix
    1 ounce cranberry juice
    1 ounce orange juice
    1 ounce pineapple juice

Pour over ice into a collins glass. Garnish with an orange slice and cherry.

Sea Breeze

*T*here's nothing quite as pleasant as a little sea breeze. Raise the sails, pull up the anchor, "cheers," and away you go.

    1½ ounces vodka
    4 ounces cranberry juice
    1 ounce grapefruit juice

Pour into a highball glass over ice cubes. Garnish with a wedge of lime.

Tropical Iced Tea

*T*he perfect recipe for when you want to clean out the liquor cabinet, or just to show off with mucho ingredients in one specialty drink. Iced tea has nothing to do with it.

½ ounce vodka
½ ounce rum
½ ounce gin
½ ounce triple sec
1 ounce sour mix
1 ounce pineapple juice
1 ounce cranberry juice
½ ounce grenadine

Combine all ingredients in mixing glass, and pour over ice in a collins glass. Garnish with seasonal fruits.

Top Banana

*A*fter all, if you're going to be a banana, why not be the top banana? This potion will help you get on top of the world. Courage. Passion. Lots of ice trays.

1 ounce vodka
1 ounce crème de banana
juice of ½ orange

Shake with ice, and strain into an old-fashioned glass over ice cubes.

Gin

*Y*ou know the line: "Of all the gin joints in all the towns in all the world, she walks into mine." Gin makes people say that kind of thing.

A clean refreshing alcohol with fruity and herbaceous overtones (okay, so this sounds like an ad for aftershave), gin is distilled from grain, then reprocessed and redistilled with various herbs and spices, primarily juniper berries (*jenever* in Dutch, thus the eventual name gin). It has been called both "Mother's ruin" and "Mother's milk."

Like most really interesting mothers, gin has a rather controversial past. It was invented as a curative several hundred years ago by a Dutch chemist who actually thought juniper berries could help treat kidney problems (this should encourage you to always get a second opinion, be it for hair color or medical treatments).

Born to travel, gin was triumphantly brought to England by British soldiers (closet bartenders at heart) who were fighting the wars in The Netherlands in the seventeenth century and caught wind of what they called "Dutch Courage." Soon the British were curing their livers and making their own curative, opening gin palaces, and exporting London gin to all their colonies.

In the eighteenth century, gin was sweetened; hence the term "London dry gin," which denotes the style, not the wit, of a dry, as opposed to sweet, gin. And let's remember to hail to the chief, the martini, whose invention elevated gin to immortal status.

Tom Collins

A little of this juniper juice goes a long way toward loosening the tongues of every Tom, Dick, and Harry.

    2 ounces gin
    juice of ½ lemon
    1 teaspoon powdered sugar
    club soda

Shake first three ingredients with ice, and strain into a collins glass. Add several ice cubes, fill glass with club soda, and stir. Decorate with slices of lemon and orange and a cherry. Serve with a straw.

Singapore Sling

*I*nvented at Raffles, a *très soigné* Singapore hotel at which any writer worth his margarita salt hung out at the bar to drink and be inspired. The bartender's quest was to create a tropical drink using something other than rum, sweet enough to please ladies but potent enough to make them giggly, which would attract men, which would provide stories for writers, and so on.

    2 ounces gin
    1 ounce cherry brandy
    1 ounce lemon juice
    soda water

Combine gin, cherry brandy, lemon juice, and cracked ice in shaker, and mix well. Strain into a large goblet or a tall glass of ice cubes. Fill with soda water. Garnish with slices

of lemon and orange, a maraschino cherry, and a sprig
of mint.

Bitch on Wheels

*N*ot named after yours truly. Invented at Stars in San
Francisco, this is the drink to serve when she (yes, you know
who) starts pulling that drama-trauma queen act *again*. Offer her
one for the road, then roll her out the front door and out of your
life. But just remember, sugar, those wheels roll both ways.

1 ounce Bombay gin
¼ ounce Martini & Rossi extra
   dry vermouth
¼ ounce Pernod
¼ ounce white crème de menthe

*Shake ingredients with ice, and strain into a chilled cocktail
glass.*

Midori Sun of a Beach

*N*ot to be left out, because there are also certain men, maybe
not on wheels, but who can be—well, you know. Muse likes to
kill them softly with kindness. On the beach. Ply them with
these and let them lie in the hot sun. Smile sweetly as you offer
yet another.

1 ounce Beefeater gin
1 ounce Midori
6 ounces orange juice

Combine over ice cubes in a tall glass.

Gin and Tonic

A classic. Savvy British servicemen in India used tonic water to take their malaria medicine, and soon discovered that a little refreshing gin also helped the medicine go down. Chalk up another great drink to medicine.

2 ounces gin
4 ounces tonic water

Pour gin into a highball glass over ice cubes and fill with tonic water. Stir. Swat the mosquitoes and sip.

Gin and Sin

*M*use thinks this a perfect combination. Not only does it rhyme, but it must be done in this order. Really now, couldn't you be just a tad more naughty?

1 ounce gin
1 ounce lemon juice
1 tablespoon orange juice
1 dash grenadine

Shake with ice, and strain into a chilled cocktail glass.

Papaya Sling

*P*apaya is good for you (all that vitamin C), and we know all about the medicinal properties of gin. Is that the glow of good health I detect? My, you can stagger far and wide when healthy, can't you?

1½ ounces gin
1 dash bitters
juice of 1 lime
1 tablespoon papaya syrup
4 ounces club soda

Shake first four ingredients with ice, and strain into a collins glass over ice cubes. Fill with club soda, and stir. Add a pineapple stick.

Extra Dry Martini

The totally urban cocktail, and one Muse's father takes to a new art form. Muse prefers hers stirred rather than shaken, despite what that devastatingly sexy secret agent demands. Shaking not only bruises the vermouth (gin doesn't bruise, honey), but those little flecks of ice chip off into the drink and dilute a perfectly potent cocktail guaranteed to render all limbs pleasantly numb.

2 ounces gin
very little dry vermouth, certainly not more than ¼ ounce

Stir gin and vermouth over ice cubes in a mixing glass. Strain into a chilled cocktail glass. Serve with three olives. Don't tell my father, but we shall spear these on a frilly toothpick.

Honolulu Hurricane Martini

Hurricanes sweep across Hawaii between tsunamis, devastating whole islands. This martini is capable of the same effects as its namesake, but Muse knows you shall sip this with nary a hair out of place, you windswept beautiful thing, you.

    4 ounces dry gin
    1 ounce French vermouth
    1 ounce Italian vermouth
    1 teaspoon pineapple juice

Shake with ice, and strain into a chilled cocktail glass.

Blue Moon

*T*he saying is once in a...but really, shouldn't we make it a bit more often?

    1½ ounces gin
    ¾ ounce blue curaçao

Stir with ice and strain into a chilled cocktail glass. Add a twist of lemon peel.

Honolulu Cocktail

*I*t is said the missionaries went to Hawaii to do good, and they did very well. Serve this drink to guests and you'll do well too. Well, you can only hope. Say a prayer and pour.

    1½ ounces gin
    1 dash bitters
    ¼ teaspoon orange juice
    ¼ teaspoon pineapple juice
    ¼ teaspoon lemon juice
    ½ teaspoon powdered sugar

Shake with ice, and strain into a chilled cocktail glass.

Hula-Hula Cocktail

*J*ust the ticket when reality seems a bit on the grim side. Slip on an aloha shirt and slip into this drink. Can you say "aloha"?

    1½ ounces gin
    ¼ ounce orange juice
    ¼ teaspoon powdered sugar

Shake with ice, and strain into a chilled cocktail glass.

MIXED DRINKS

Bourbon & Whiskey

*L*ife can be confusing at times, which is why we have cocktails to relieve the pressure. But then there's "whiskey" and "whisky" and "bourbon," and it can become oh so confusing again. Muse will try to clarify.

Bourbon whiskey was created in Kentucky some 200 years ago and is America's only native spirit. The state still produces 80 percent of the world's bourbon, which is distilled from a mash of grain containing at least 51 percent corn, along with barley and wheat or rye. Bourbon's amber color and pleasant sweetness come from aging a minimum of two years in new white oak barrels whose interiors have been charred, to cast off the natural sugars in the wood. Yummy.

Tennessee whiskey, such as Jack Daniel's, is often called bourbon, but legally (yes, there are laws for important matters such as these) Tennessee whiskey is in a class by itself due to one unique step in the distilling process. Before barreling, the bourbon is "mellowed," or slowly filtered, through sugar maple charcoal, giving it a signature smoky-sweet flavor.

Scotch whisky is produced exclusively in Scotland where the peat (thus its smoky flavor), water, and shape of the still are highly influential. Irish whiskey is produced only in Ireland, and the malt is dried in kilns so there is no smoky flavor. American whiskeys are either straight (distilled from a single grain) or blended; and Canadian whisky, made only in Canada, is usually lighter-tasting than its American counterpart. Whew, Muse now needs a drink.

Mint Julep

With these frosty silver cups of pleasure in tow, you'll see the bluegrass grow, those Kentucky Derby horses will run just a tad faster, and you'll be off to the races in no time.

    5 sprigs of mint
    ¼ ounce sugar syrup
    2½ ounces bourbon

In a silver cup, muddle 4 mint sprigs with sugar syrup. Fill with crushed ice and add bourbon. Stir until silver cup is quite heavily frosted. Garnish with mint sprig and a short straw.

7 Seas

Never sailed the seven seas? Pity, but you can get some very good mileage out of this cocktail, which is sure to enhance drifting.

    1½ ounces Seagram's 7 whiskey
    ½ ounce melon liqueur
    ½ ounce pineapple juice

Combine over ice.

California Lemonade

A pitcher of these citrus delights will inspire California dreamin' on the stormiest of days. Do you know the way to San Jose?

2 ounces blended whiskey
¼ teaspoon grenadine
juice of 1 lemon
juice of 1 lime
1 tablespoon powdered sugar
4 ounces club soda

Shake first five ingredients with ice and strain into a collins glass over shaved ice. Fill with club soda and decorate with slices of orange and lemon, and a cherry. Serve with straws.

Dixie Whiskey Cocktail

This is one rather potent drink, and I'm not just whistlin' Dixie. Stand back and shake. Then watch those Dixie cups dance.

2 ounces bourbon
½ teaspoon powdered sugar
1 dash bitters
¼ teaspoon triple sec
½ teaspoon white crème de menthe

Shake with ice, and strain into a cocktail glass.

Tequila & Mescal

*I*t's not easy being real tequila. You must be from Mexico, born in one of two specific regions. You're distilled from the sugary sap of the cooked heart of the mature Weber blue agave (pronounced *uh-gah-vay*) plant (sometimes called a century plant) which has first matured ten years before offering its heart up to be ground and heated. Only blue agave can be used for tequila, which must contain at least 51 percent agave juice—it's the law. The best tequilas are 100 percent agave and are certified as such.

Like rum, tequila comes in several shades. White tequila is ready for export after distillation; gold is aged in white oak casks for two to four years; tequila añejo is aged for at least one year. And it goes on from there.

Muse highly recommends NORMA-approved tequila. Some of you may think you know her, but NORMA isn't just any girl; she's the defining señorita of the Mexican government. Real tequila that has met the government's tough requirements will have NOM followed by four numbers on the distiller's label. Trust me, it's the NORMA rating, and you want NORMA or nothing.

While every tequila is a mescal, not every mescal is a tequila. Spelled *mezcal* in Mexico, it too is distilled from the blue agave plant in the state of Oaxaca, but the process is different, and some distillers place an agave worm in the bottle to denote its authenticity. But, Muse asks, unless you know an agave worm from, say, an earthworm, what good is it?

Under the Volcano Martini

*I*t's not that hot in San Francisco, where Harry Denton of the Starlight Room invented this drink above the skyline, but this martini will warm your bones as if you were under a volcano, instead of teetering on the edge of the San Andreas like Harry.

  2 ounces mescal
  ½ ounce Martini & Rossi vermouth

Stir over ice in a cocktail glass. Garnish with a jalapeño-stuffed olive.

Margarita

*J*immy Buffet took many of us to "Margaritaville," a torrid tropical island to waste away on. Buy your own ticket to Margaritaville with this potion and don't come back until you're ready.

  rind of a lemon or lime
  coarse salt
  2 ounces tequila
  ½ ounce triple sec
  1 ounce lemon or lime juice

Rub rim of a cocktail glass with rind of lemon or lime. Dip rim in coarse salt. Shake remaining ingredients with ice, and strain into salt-rimmed glass.

Coconut Almond Margarita

*T*his delightful margarita is coco-licious. Better get the mariachi band over here, because two of these bambinos make a party!

1¼ ounces Jose Cuervo 1800 tequila
2½ ounces sweet-and-sour mix
½ ounce cream of coconut
¼ ounce amaretto
½ ounce fresh lime juice

Shake, and serve over ice (for a frozen concoction, blend with crushed ice). Garnish with a wedge of lime.

Tequila Sunrise

*W*ake up and smell the tequila—it's never too early.

2 ounces tequila
4 ounces orange juice
¼ ounce grenadine

Pour tequila over ice in glass. Stir in orange juice. Add grenadine. Garnish with a slice of orange and a cherry. Serve with a straw. If you prefer a Tequila Sunset, simply stir before serving.

Bloody Maria

*M*exico has its own Bloody Mary, probably renowned for breaking men's hearts. Take solace in this drink the morning after the object of your latest *affaire de coeur* has left you and your shaker for a snappier Tomás.

1 ounce tequila
2 ounces tomato juice
1 dash lemon juice
1 dash Tabasco sauce
1 dash celery salt

Shake all ingredients with cracked ice. Strain into an old-fashioned glass over ice cubes. Add a slice of lemon.

Pacific Sunshine

*T*he sun is always shining somewhere over the blue, calm Pacific. Unleash golden rays of sunshine in your head with this potion.

lemon or lime rind
coarse salt
1½ ounces tequila
1½ ounces blue curaçao
1½ ounces sour mix
1 dash bitters

Rub the rim of a chilled parfait or hurricane glass with lemon or lime rind, invert glass, and dip rim in salt till nicely coated. Mix remaining ingredients with cracked ice and pour, with ice, into glass. Garnish with a lemon wheel.

Purple Gecko

*M*use rather likes the buggy-eyed creatures who can walk up and down walls, especially dressed in purple like this wild cocktail.

- 1½ ounces tequila
- ½ ounce blue curaçao
- ½ ounce red curaçao
- 1 ounce cranberry juice
- 1 ounce sour mix
- ½ ounce lime juice

Shake with ice, and pour into a salt-rimmed cocktail or margarita glass. Garnish with a lime wedge.

Mexicana

*Y*ou'll fly across the border, plane or no plane, with a good bottle of mescal. Now, for whom does the worm toll?

- 1¼ ounces mescal
- ¾ ounce lemon or lime juice
- 1½ ounces pineapple juice
- 1 splash grenadine

Mix all ingredients in shaker with 1 scoop crushed ice. Fill a highball glass with fresh crushed ice, and strain shaker contents over it.

Shots

*M*ademoiselle posits that aquavit was the world's first jazzy shooter. Sometime in the 15th century, someone had the brilliant idea to flavor cheap, rough vodka with caraway seeds (later variations included cumin, cardamon, aniseed, fennel, lemon and orange peel). This Scandinavian flavored and distilled liquor is served well-chilled and straight up in small glasses that should be emptied in one shot.

You may recall that redhead barmaid, Miss Kitty, of *Gunsmoke*, who oversaw many a whiskey poured into a shot glass and knocked back in a giant swallow by dusty cowboys and tall sheriffs. A bit later in the century, working-class bars served a variation of this shooter known as The Boilermaker or Depthcharge—a mug of cold beer and a shot of vodka or whiskey. Some men would shoot the liquor, then down the beer as a chaser. Others would mix the two together. However, for a Depthcharge, the shot glass of liquor is dropped into the beer and the whole thing is chugged…not unlike the contemporary Flaming Dr Pepper.

Today's honky tonk bars find urban cowboys downing shots of tequila, bookended with a lick of salt and a suck on a lime wedge. "Shots," "shooters," "slammers"…call them what you will, these teeny-weeny glasses (sometimes in kitschy shapes) filled with a bit of alcohol and juice or mixer are so fun and amusing. Muse absolutely adores them. Here's a chance to be totally creative on a smaller scale. Mix or layer potions for effect. Pass a tray of these around when things get dull. Perhaps these are all you need?

Flaming Dr Pepper

I owe this fiery concoction to my fellow cocktail charmers Simon and Baron, two snappy young gentlemen— secure enough in their masculinity to wear little paper umbrellas behind their ears— who are quite generous in sharing their Ever Clear vision of life, gallantly pulled from a silver flask, when a club's drinks don't quite measure up to Muse's standards. If you see them, ask for some.

1. Fill a shot glass with amaretto.
2. Top the shot with Ever Clear.
3. Light it.
4. Drop the flaming shot glass into a pint of beer.
5. Chug it.

Mind Eraser

*A*nother concoction from those infamous men on the town, Simon and Baron. In the confessional booth at The Irish Bank (truly, a bar in San Francisco), they divulged the ingredients to this mind smasher.

1 part vodka
1 part Kahlua
1 part club soda

Shake with ice, and strain into a shot glass.

B-52 with Bombay Doors

*T*his will have you flying. Just make sure the doors are open when you're ready to jump.

    1 part Bombay gin
    1 part Kahlua
    1 part Bailey's Irish Cream
    1 part Grand Marnier

Shake with ice, and strain into a shot glass.

The Parisian Blonde

*I*nterested in the foreign service? The foreign accent? The French are such seductive little vixens. Take one to the Caribbean and this is what happens...they get mixed up with not one, but two rums. Ooh la la!

    ¼ ounce light rum
    ¼ ounce triple sec
    ¼ ounce Jamaican dark rum

Shake with ice, and strain into a cordial glass. Affect an accent and serve to blondes only.

Bandera

*F*or this international favorite, Cocktail Muse did some heavy research in Mexico and uncovered this drink named for the colors of the Mexican flag: green (lime juice), red (tomato juice), and white (tequila).

1 shot glass real tequila
1 shot glass spicy tomato or Clamato juice
1 shot glass fresh lime juice

Sip or shoot each in succession.

To the Moon

"Fly me to the moon," crooned Sinatra. And, indeed, you might just get there in your mind, with enough of these slammers. Batten down the hatch because it's blastoff time!

½ ounce Irish cream liqueur
½ ounce amaretto
½ ounce coffee liqueur
½ ounce 151-proof rum

Combine in a shot glass.

TWA High

This gem of a high-flying drink came to Muse from frequent-flyer friends who commute to San Francisco to see the opera. Yes it's that good…the drink and the opera. While the former benefits from high altitude, the latter is best appreciated from non-nosebleed seats that are closer to the *Sturm und Drang* of the performance. However, I wonder if it is not this drink that keeps my friends and their points quite high.

2 ounces Grand Marnier
2 ounces Bailey's Irish Cream

Serve in a first-class glass over crushed ice (optional) and garnish with a flourish of whipped cream and a cherry.

Glossary

Bottoms Up—Depending on the number of libations one has consumed, this could mean one thing or another. We'll assume here it's "another," which refers to draining the glass in hand, requiring that the drinker tilt the bottom of the glass upward, the liquid emptying into the open mouth.

A Float—A liquor poured on top of the drink, floating, thus making a cameo appearance. Usually a float is brandy or 151 rum, which is so strong that it comes with its own pourer. Unless devilish you want to be floating immediately, use the pourer.

Muddle—You might find yourself in a muddle, or muddle your head with too many kitschy libations, but really you should just muddle the sugar in a glass with the muddler, a nifty wooden pestle.

On the Rocks—The bartender is not interested in your love life, but merely is asking if you want ice cubes.

A Pour—As in "pour me more, por favor." But the verb changeth into a noun with the article attached. A pour is a measured quantity; bars usually have devices on bottles to dispense just the right amount of booze—no more, no less.

Shaker Style—The inimitable style and magic with which you, bartender extraordinaire, twirl, shake, rattle, and roll that cocktail shaker. Warning: Some neophytes might think you are referring to a furniture style *très* devoid of kitsch.

Straight Up—Refers not to posture, but to a drink served with no ice.

Index

About the Author

$\mathcal{B}$abs Harrison has been preparing for the cocktail hour most of her life. She grew up in Texas (where her father instructed her in the mechanics of the perfect martini), attended school in Virginia (learning the necessity of tradition), lived in France (wine tastings and cooking classes, and the importance of wearing high heels), and Hawaii (intense tropical drink and pupu research). A former food writer for *The Dallas Morning News*, her previous books include *The Lion in the Moon: Two Against the Sahara*, *Exploring New Mexico Wine Country*, and the companion to this book, *Kitschy Canapés: Finger Foods for the Swinger Set*. She and her cocktail shaker currently swing in San Francisco.